The Pho
Cookbook

50 Easy to Creative Recipes for Vietnam's Favorite Soup and Noodles

Mathias Müller

Images: Fotolia
Copy-Editing, Proofreading: Mathias Müller

Published by:
Mathias Müller
Woltmanstraße 10
20097 Hamburg

ISBN-13: 978-1974496945

ISBN-10: 1974496945

TABLE OF CONTENTS

INTRODUCTION 6

Pho Noodles Soup Base.. 8

    Basic Pho Base 8

    Beef Pho Base 10

    Chicken Pho Base 11

    Vegetable Pho Base 12

Heavy Authentic Pho Noodles.. 14

    Protein Rich Vietnam Pho Noodles 14

    Chicken and Mushroom Pho 15

    Quick Thanksgiving Leftover Pho 16

    Sweet Seafood Breakfast Pho 18

    Authentic Southern Vietnamese Pho 19

    Spicy Beef Pho 20

    Meatballs Pho 21

    Fish Pho Soup 22

    Grilled Pork Pho.. 24

    Sweet and Sour Shrimp Pho 25

Light and Medium Authentic Pho... 27

    It Thit Pho Bo 27

    It Thit Pho Ga 28

    Not so Beef Pho (Less Noodle Beef Pho)....................... 29

    Not so Chicken Pho... 30

    Egg Pho Chay (Vegetable Pho with Egg)........................ 31

    Beef Tripe Pho 32

    Pho Bo Chay.. 33

    It Pho Ga (Less Soup Rice Noodle)................................. 34

Vegan Pho Noodles 36

    Spiced Tofu and Mushroom Pho 36

    Vietnamese Vegetable Pho 37

Poor Man's Pho 38

Quick Vegetable Pho 39

Zucchini Pho.. 40

Calabash (Bottle Gourd) and Sprouts Pho....................... 41

Spicy Vegan Pho... 43

Tay Pho 44

Winter Pho Chay.. 45

Sour Vegetable Pho 46

Pho with a Twist 48

Imperial Beef Noodle Soup.. 48

Pork Feet Ginseng Pho... 49

Mexican Influenced Pho 51

Bat Choy (Filipino Style Pho)... 52

Boiled Down Tofu over Pho 53

Ravioli in Pho Broth 54

Sour and Spicy Pho 56

Phorridge 57

Other Vietnamese Noodle Soups 58

Duck Noodle Soup with Bamboo Shoots.......................... 58

Bun Bo Hue 59

Bun Riu or Tomato Noodle Soup 61

Cucumber Noodle Soup.. 62

Rice Pasta with Pork and Shrimp Sticks 63

Pho and Noodle Partners.. 65

Vietnamese Spring Rolls 65

Bahn Tieu (Hollow Donuts).. 66

Quay or Fried Bread Sticks... 67

Steamed Sweet Rice Cake 68

Banh Goi or Crispy Dumplings 69

CONCLUSION 71

AUTHOR.. 72

INTRODUCTION

Pho is one of the famous noodle soups in Asia and the top favorite noodle soup in Vietnam. It is also listed as one of the 50 most delicious foods in the world.

This delicious dish is offered as a street food in Vietnam. It is usually sold at dawn and at dusk. Many Vietnamese would have them for breakfast or for dinner. Nonetheless, it is a dish that can be eaten any time of the day.

Pho is popular among Vietnamese locals and tourists because it is a complete and satisfying meal in a bowl. It is has a mix of vegetables, meat, and carbohydrates. It is often served with beef or chicken and rice noodles. Also, since it is made from natural ingredients, the flavor and the taste are wonderful treats for everyone's taste buds.

Some people think that it is just another Asian soup, like the ramen of Japan. But, Pho is quite different from most Asian soups. What sets it apart is the broth. The broths used in the recipes are natural. They do not use any artificial flavor or pre-made seasonings. The broth is a product of long hours of slow cooking without any additives.

All the ingredients in the Pho are required to be fresh for it to be delicious and healthy. Its preparation requires time. This is why Pho noodle soups cannot be replicated in instant noodle variants.

With the help of this book, it would be easy for you to enjoy a hearty bowl of Pho. Make some Vietnamese dumplings and donuts to eat with your Pho and you will have one satisfying meal.

Another interesting fact about Pho is its flexibility. Each person can choose and add different seasonings according to his preference. The noodle soup can be spicy, sweet, meaty, or sour.

The broth is also versatile enough to be used in many different recipes. The broth has less fat and can easily absorb the taste of the added meat and vegetables. It is a soup that allows you to be creative according to your taste. This is why Vietnamese and many people in the world could not get enough of Pho noodle soups.

Pho Noodles Soup Base

Reminder: Be careful when adding salt. The moment you taste a hint of salt, stop adding the seasoning. Pho is traditionally served with sauces that can make your broth saltier.

The broth can last in the fridge for three days and 2 weeks, if frozen. Simmer the beef bones longer, if you want to freeze it. Freezing tends to make the soup bland.

The number of servings is mentioned in Directions.

Basic Pho Base

Nutritional facts per serving:
Calories: 31.1kcal
Fat: 1.7g
Protein: 2.2g
Carbohydrates: 2g
Fiber: less than 1g

Ingredients:
- 2 kilos beef bones
- 1 kilo free range chicken, chopped into large pieces
- 1 kilo beef shanks
- 6 to 8 star anise, depending on size
- 2 pieces of dried cardamom
- 1 cinnamon stick
- fish sauce

- salt
- 4 medium whole shallots
- ginger (about the size of three fingers), peeled
- water
- 1 tablespoon brown sugar or 1" cubed rock sugar, optional

Directions:

1. Boil 16 cups of water. Add the beef bones and simmer for 30 minutes on medium heat. Add the beef shanks and simmer for another hour. Skim off the foam every 10 minutes.
2. Toast the star anise, cardamom and cinnamon for 1 minute on low heat. Remove from fire and wash. Put in the pot.
3. Add the chicken. Stir in three tablespoons of fish sauce and 1 tablespoon of salt.
4. Smash the ginger. Add to the pot and cook the broth for 1 hour or until the beef shanks are tender. Skim the foam every 10 minutes and remove the excess oil on the surface.
5. Remove the beef shanks from the pot and separate the meat from the bones. Return the bones to the pot. Set aside the meat.
6. Smash the shallots and add to the broth. Simmer for 30 minutes. Add the sugar. Stir in more fish sauce or salt to correct the taste.
7. Pour the hot broth over your prepared noodles. You can also let the broth cool down overnight to allow the excess fat to solidify. Take out the fat and reheat the broth before using. Makes 8 to 10 servings.

Beef Pho Base

Nutritional facts per serving:
Calories: 26.7kcal
Fat: 1.4g
Protein: 1.9g
Carbohydrates: 2g
Fiber: less than 1g

Ingredients:
- All ingredients for the basic Pho Soup Base except for the chicken
- 1 tablespoon brown sugar (now required)
- 3 cloves

Directions:
1. Boil the bones and 20 cups of water on high heat for 30 minutes. Turn down the fire to medium and add the shanks. Simmer for 1 hour. Skim the foam and remove the fat on the surface.
2. Add 3 tablespoons of fish sauce, 2 tablespoons of salt, and crushed ginger.
3. Toast the cardamom, cinnamon, clove, and star anise. Wash and add to the broth. Continue to cook for another hour. Skim the foam and remove the fat every 10 minutes.
4. Add the smashed shallots and sugar. Boil for another 30 minutes. Season more, if needed. Pour over noodles or set aside until the excess fat solidifies. Serves 10 to 12.

Chicken Pho Base

Nutritional facts per serving:
Calories: 18kcal
Fat: 1.4g
Protein: 1.3g
Carbohydrates: 2g
Fiber: less than 1g

Ingredients:
- 4 large free range chicken or 6 kilos of whole legs
- ginger, about the size of 3 fingers, peeled and smashed
- 4 shallots, smashed
- 1 cinnamon stick
- 2 thin slices of licorice root
- 1 tablespoon light brown sugar
- fish sauce
- salt
- 1 clove garlic, smashed (optional, not recommended if you want to preserve the soup)

Directions:
1. Boil 15 cups of water in a large pot. Add all the chicken. Reduce heat to medium and simmer for 45 minutes. Skim the foam every 10 minutes.
2. Add the smashed ginger, 3 tablespoons of fish sauce, and 1 tablespoon of salt. Toast the cinnamon, shallots, and licorice. Add to the broth. Simmer for another 30 minutes. Skim the foam and remove the excess fat.
3. Turn off the heat and set aside to allow the fat to rise. Remove the excess fat. Serves 8 to 10.

Vegetable Pho Base

<u>Nutritional facts per serving:</u>
Calories: 5 kcal
Fat: less than 1g
Protein: less than 1g
Carbohydrates: 2g
Fiber: less than 1g

<u>Ingredients:</u>
- 16 cups of water
- 1 large daikon radish, peeled
- 1 large sweet corn cob
- 2 large carrots, peeled
- 2 large apples or pears
- 1 large leek
- 1 large onion
- ginger, about three fingers big
- 2 large shallots
- 1 cinnamon stick
- 2 dried cardamoms
- 1 thin slice of licorice root
- 3 star anise
- 1 tablespoon light brown sugar or 1 1" rock sugar
- 3 tablespoons light soy sauce
- 1 tablespoon salt

Directions:
1. Place the shallots, ginger, cardamoms, licorice, cinnamon, and anise on a baking sheet. Bake at 200C for 20 minutes. Wash and set aside.
2. Cut the vegetables in large slices. As for the leeks, slice the white part thinly.

3. Boil 16 cups of water in a large pot. Add all the vegetables, seasonings, and spices. Simmer for 45 minutes. Taste. Add more soy sauce if needed.

4. Remove from fire and pour over the noodles immediately.

Heavy Authentic Pho Noodles

Protein Rich Vietnam Pho Noodles

Nutritional facts per serving:
Calories: 509 kcal
Fat: 11g
Protein: 37g
Carbohydrates: 77g
Fiber: 4.7 g

Ingredients:
- 6 to 8 cups of basic Pho broth
- 300 grams wide rice noodles or 400 grams thin rice noodles
- 200 grams beef sirloin, excess fats trimmed, sliced thinly
- 200 grams cooked chicken breast, cut into medium sized chunks
- ½ cup onions, sliced thinly
- a handful of coriander, chopped
- 6 spring onions, chopped thinly
- 10 to 12 basil, chopped
- 1 lime, quartered
- 2 tablespoons of hoisin sauce
- 1 tablespoon of chili sauce (optional)
- slivers of red chili pepper (optional)
- salt and black pepper

Directions:

1. Boil 4 cups of water in a bowl. Drop the rice noodles in the briskly boiling water. Immediately drain the noodles. Divide into 4 portions and place each portion to separate bowls.
2. Divide the onion, sirloin and chicken into the bowls. Combine the coriander, spring onion and basil. Distribute equally to the number of bowls.
3. Reheat the broth. Cover the noodles with briskly boiling broth. Squeeze the juice of one lime wedge over the broth.
4. Top with hoisin sauce, chili sauce and slices of red chili pepper. Add salt and pepper, if necessary.

Chicken and Mushroom Pho

Nutritional facts per serving:
Calories: 243 kcal
Fat: 6.4g
Protein: 17.1g
Carbohydrates: 37g
Fiber: 2.1g

Ingredients:
- 6 cups of the chicken Pho soup base
- 2 breasts of chicken, you may use the breast of chicken from the chicken you used for the broth
- 1 cup mushroom, sliced
- ¾ cup onion, sliced
- 1 clove garlic
- ¼ cup chopped cilantro
- ¼ cup spring onion
- ¼ cup hoisin sauce
- 1 green chili pepper, seeded and sliced thinly
- 1 teaspoon vegetable oil
- 300 grams wide rice noodles

- salt and pepper
- lime

Directions:
1. Place a skillet over medium heat. Sauté ¼ cup onion in oil for three minutes. Stir in the garlic and cook for 2 minutes. Add the mushrooms and sauté for 2 minutes.
2. Add 2 tablespoons of chicken broth. Reduce the fire to low and cook for 5 minutes.
3. Meanwhile, boil water in a deep pot. Drop the rice noodles in briskly boiling hot water and immediately drain the water. Distribute into 4 bowls.
4. Chop the chicken and distribute it equally to each bowl. Remove the mushroom from fire and let it cool. Distribute it and the onion to each of the bowl.
5. Combine the cilantro and spring onion. Add them to the bowl.
6. Bring the broth to boil and pour over the noodles. Serve with hoisin sauce, chili pepper and lime.

Quick Thanksgiving Leftover Pho

Nutritional facts per serving:
Calories: 231 kcal
Fat: 5.4g
Protein: 16.3g
Carbohydrates: 33g
Fiber: 1.9g

Ingredients:
- 300 grams wide rice noodles or glass noodles
- 2 cups roasted turkey leftover, chopped
- 2 cups water
- 6 cups chicken stock
- ¼ cup ginger, sliced

- 3 star anise
- 1 tablespoon apple-cider vinegar
- 3 tablespoons fish sauce
- 2 tablespoons honey or 1 tablespoon light brown sugar
- ½ cup onion, sliced
- 3 gloves garlic, minced
- a handful of basil, chopped roughly
- ½ cup of cilantro, chopped roughly
- ¼ cup leeks, white part only, sliced thinly
- ¼ cup leeks, green part only, chopped finely
- 1 cup mushroom, sliced
- 2 tablespoon olive oil
- juice of 1 lime
- salt and pepper

Directions:

1. Place a pot over medium-high heat. Add oil and sauté the onion and the white part of leeks for 3 minutes. Add the garlic and mushroom. Cook for 5 minutes.
2. Add the turkey and sauté for three minutes. Pour in the water and chicken stock. Bring to a boil.
3. Place the ginger and the star anise in a tea bag or tea case and drop it in the stock. Mix in the fish sauce, vinegar and sugar. Bring to a quick boil and simmer for 20 minutes.
4. Add the basil, cilantro and the green part of leeks. Save some for garnishing.
5. Season with salt and pepper. Add the lime juice and turn off the heat.
6. Cook the rice noodle or glass noodle according to package instruction. Divide into 4 to 5 bowls.
7. Scoop the broth over the noodles. Distribute the turkey and other ingredients to each bowl. Garnish with the remaining basil, cilantro and leeks.

Sweet Seafood Breakfast Pho

Nutritional facts per serving:
Calories: 157 kcal
Fat: 2g
Protein: 7g
Carbohydrates: 28g
Fiber: 4.4g

Ingredients:
- 6 cups of vegetable pho broth
- 2 large pears, peeled
- 1 medium daikon radish, peeled
- ½ cup cilantro
- ½ cup of basil
- 12 to 16 prawns, peeled, deveined and chopped
- ¼ cup onion
- 1 teaspoon fried garlic
- 250 to 300 grams thin rice noodles, cooked
- 1 lime, sliced into wedges
- 1 green chili pepper, sliced thinly

Directions:
1. Distribute the cooked noodles to 4 or 5 bowls. Scoop equal amounts of chopped prawn for each bowls. Distribute the onion, cilantro and basil to each bowls, too.
2. Slice the pear and radish into thin slices. Place on top of the noodles.
3. Pour the boiling broth over the noodles. Top with a few fried garlic and chili pepper. Serve with lime.

Authentic Southern Vietnamese Pho

Nutritional facts per serving:

Calories: 509 kcal

Fat: 11g

Protein: 35g

Carbohydrates: 64g

Fiber: 4.4g

Ingredients:

- 400 grams of thin rice noodles
- 8 cups of beef Pho soup or basic Pho soup
- 1½ cup mung bean sprouts, blanched
- 1 cup onion
- 1 cup cilantro, chopped
- 1 cup spring onions, chopped
- 200 grams sirloin steak, cut into thin strips
- basil twigs for garnish
- lime wedges
- hoisin sauce
- Tabasco hot sauce
- sweet chili sauce
- salt and pepper
- slices of green chili pepper

Directions:

1. Distribute the cook noodles in 4 to 6 bowls. Arrange slices of raw sirloin steak strips in one portion of the bowl.
2. Arrange the bean sprouts, onion, cilantro and spring onion on top of the noodles.
3. Bring the broth to a boil and ladle over to the prepared noodle bowl. Serve with any of the sauce, lime or chili pepper.

Spicy Beef Pho

Nutritional facts per serving:
Calories: 567 kcal
Fat: 14g
Protein: 35g
Carbohydrates: 67g
Fiber: 3.7g

Ingredients:
- 1 kilo beef brisket
- 3 kilos beef bones
- 4 star anise, depending on size
- 2 pieces of dried cardamom
- 1 cinnamon stick
- fish sauce
- salt
- 4 medium whole shallots
- ginger (about the size of three fingers)
- 1 tablespoon brown sugar or 1 1" cubed rock sugar, optional
- Water
- 2 tablespoons dried pepper flakes
- Garlic
- 1 cup onion
- 1 cup chopped cilantro
- ¼ cup green onions
- hot sauce
- 2 tablespoons olive oil
- 500 grams wide rice noodles

Directions:
1. Boil 16 cups of water in a deep pot. Put the beef bones and brisket in the pot and simmer on medium heat for 2 hours.

2. Add 4 tablespoons of fish sauce and 1 tablespoon each of salt and rock sugar.
3. Heat the oil in a small skillet. Add the dried pepper flakes and sauté in low heat for 2 minutes. Increase the fire to medium and add the smashed shallots and ginger. Sauté for 5 minutes. Add the pepper mixture to the pot of beef.
4. In the same skillet, place the cardamom, anise, and cinnamon stick. Roast in the oven at 200 degrees C for 10 minutes. Rinse the toasted spices before adding them to the beef. Cook for another hour.
5. Cook the rice noodles according to instructions or as done in the previous recipes. Distribute among 6 to 8 bowls.
6. Slice the beef thinly and place equal amounts in each bowl. Top with onions and cilantro.
7. Pour the spicy broth over the noodles. Serve with hot sauce and lime wedges.

Meatballs Pho

Nutritional facts per serving:
Calories: 312 kcal
Fat: 12g
Protein: 34g
Carbohydrates: 29g
Fiber: 1.2g

Ingredients:
- 200 grams 90% lean ground beef
- 1 cup finely minced boiled beef shank (the same shank used for the broth
- ½ cup carrots
- ¼ cup minced onion
- 1 egg yolk
- 1 teaspoon bread crumbs

- ½ cup sliced onion
- ½ cup cilantro
- ½ cup green onion
- 8 cups of basic or beef Pho soup base
- steamed bean sprouts (optional)
- 400 grams thin rice noodles

Directions:

1. Cook the rice noodles. Distribute it among 6 bowls. Do not spread the noodles to the side of the bowl. Leave some space around the mound of noodles for the meatballs.
2. Combine all the beef, carrots, onion, and bread crumbs. Add the egg yolk. Shape into balls.
3. Place an equal number of meatballs in the bowls, arranging them around the noodles. Top the noodles with steamed bean sprouts, onion, cilantro, and green onions.
4. Boil the broth and pour over the noodles. Serve with hoisin or hot sauce.

Fish Pho Soup

Nutritional facts per serving:
Calories: 248 kcal
Fat: 3g
Protein: 27g
Carbohydrates: 37g
Fiber: 1.3g

Ingredients:
- 2 kilos of fish head
- 10 cups of water
- 1 cup white part of lemon grass
- 3 tablespoon fish sauce
- 1 tablespoon salt

- 1 medium daikon radish
- 2 scallions halved
- 1 cinnamon stick
- 2 star anise
- ginger, about the size of three fingers
- apple-cider vinegar
- 500 grams cod or tilapia, filleted
- 300 grams of rice noodles, thin
- 1 bunch bok choy leaves or amaranth leaves
- ½ cup scallions, sliced thinly
- 1 red chili pepper, sliced thinly
- oil

Directions:

1. Boil the water in a large pot. Add the fish head, lemon grass, halved scallions, radish, vinegar, salt, and fish sauce. Simmer over medium fire for 30 minutes.
2. Toast the ginger, anise, and cinnamon stick for 10 minutes. Rinse and add to the fish. Cook for another 25 minutes.
3. Cook the rice noodles as instructed in the package or according to the preceding recipes. Distribute among 5 bowls.
4. Heat a non-stick pan over medium fire. Add a few drops of oil and grill the fish until golden brown. Slice into cubes and arrange on top of the prepared noodles.
5. Blanch the bok choy for 10 seconds and roughly chop. Add on top of the rice noodles. Top with sliced scallions and chili pepper. Pour the broth over the noodles.

Grilled Pork Pho

Nutritional facts per serving:
Calories: 343 kcal
Fat: 8g
Protein: 33g
Carbohydrates: 47g
Fiber: 9g

Ingredients:
- 600 grams pork tenderloin
- salt and pepper
- 400 grams thin rice noodles
- 1 cup chopped cilantro
- ½ cup spring onions
- 1 cup onion
- 2 tablespoons roasted peanuts, crushed
- 1 cup mung bean sprouts, blanched

Directions:
1. Preheat oven to 200c for 10 minutes. Rub salt and pepper on the tenderloin.
2. Heat a little oil in an oven-proof pan and brown the tenderloin on all sides. Transfer the pork to the oven roaster for one hour. (You may also use leftover roast pork to skip this step.)
3. Cook the rice noodle as instructed and distribute it among 4 to 5 bowls.
4. Slice the pork into thin cubes and arrange equal amounts in each bowl. Add sprouts to the sides, if using.
5. Top with 1 teaspoon peanuts, cilantro, scallions, and spring onions. Serve with lime wedges, hoisin sauce, vinegar, or green chili pepper.

Sweet and Sour Shrimp Pho

Nutritional facts per serving:
Calories: 163 kcal
Fat: 4g
Protein: 7g
Carbohydrates: 36g
Fiber: 4g

Ingredients:
- 1 pound steamed shrimps, peeled and deveined
- ½ pound tamarind of ½ cup fresh tamarind meat
- 1 cup water
- 6 cups chicken or vegetable Pho soup base
- syrup from 16oz pineapple chunks in can
- 1 cup yellow onion, sliced
- 200 grams tofu
- 2 red bell pepper, sliced thinly
- ½ pound mung bean sprouts, blanched
- 1 cup cilantro, roughly chopped
- ½ cup green onion, chopped
- 300 grams rice noodles, wide
- pinch of Chinese five-spice or ngoyong

Directions:
1. Press the tofu between two sheets of wax paper to drain excess liquid. Slice to ½" thick and sprinkle with ngoyong. Brown the tofu in a little oil.
2. Arrange the shrimps, tofu, onion, bell pepper, and bean sprouts on top of the cooked rice noodles. Top with the combined cilantro and green onions.
3. Mix the tamarind meat and water. Remove the seeds.
4. Bring the broth to a boil. Pour in the tamarind water and the pineapple syrup. Boil for 10 minutes. Add more rock sugar, if

desired. Scoop into the bowls prepared earlier. Serve with sweet chili sauce and lime wedges.

Light and Medium Authentic Pho

It Thit Pho Bo

Nutritional facts per serving:
Calories: 197 kcal
Fat: 7.5g
Protein: 14g
Carbohydrates: 29g
Fiber: 1.3g

Ingredients:
- 400 grams rice noodles, thin
- ½ cup ground beef, 70% lean
- 1 cup mushrooms, chopped
- 1 cup yellow onion
- 10 cups basic pho soup or beef soup
- ½ cup spring onion
- lime

Directions:
1. Prepare the rice noodles as instructed. Divide among 5 cups.
2. Scoop 1 tablespoon of ground beef and place it on top of the rice noodles. Add the mushrooms and onions.

3. Slice the lime thinly and in a crosswise direction. Place two slices on top of the noodles.
4. Boil the soup and pour over the noodles.

It Thit Pho Ga

Nutritional facts per serving:
Calories: 163 kcal
Fat: 2g
Protein: 8g
Carbohydrates: 33g
Fiber: less than 1g

Ingredients:
- 400 grams rice noodles, thin
- 1 chicken breasts, boiled and shredded
- 1 cup yellow cabbage, shredded
- 1 cup yellow onion
- 10 cups chicken pho soup
- ½ cup spring onion
- ½ cup cilantro
- 1 green pepper, sliced thinly
- lime wedges

Directions:
1. Cook the rice noodles as instructed and place equal amounts in 5 bowls.
2. Arrange the shredded chicken, cabbage, onion, and the combined spring onions and cilantro.
3. Pour the boiling chicken pho soup. Serve with lime and green pepper slices.

Not so Beef Pho (Less Noodle Beef Pho)

<u>Nutritional facts per serving:</u>
Calories: 358 kcal
Fat: 15g
Protein: 32g
Carbohydrates: 14g
Fiber: less than 1g

<u>Ingredients:</u>
- 200 grams rice noodles, thin
- 400 grams sirloin steak, sliced thinly
- 2 cups bean sprouts, blanched
- 1 cup onion, sliced
- 1 cup cilantro, chopped roughly
- ½ cup spring onion
- Lime
- hoisin sauce, or chili garlic sauce
- 10 cups of basic pho or beef pho soup

Directions:
1. Cook the noodles and distribute it among 5 bowls.
2. Distribute the beef, sprouts, onion, cilantro, and spring onions. Arrange them on top of the noodles.
3. Pour the boiling soup into the bowl. Serve with lime and hoisin or chili sauce.

Not so Chicken Pho

<u>Nutritional facts per serving:</u>
Calories: 165 kcal
Fat: 4g
Protein: 17g
Carbohydrates: 9.8g
Fiber: less than 1g

<u>Ingredients:</u>
- 200 grams rice noodles, thin
- 2 cups shredded cooked chicken breasts
- 1 cup mushrooms
- 1 cup yellow onion
- 1 cup yellow cabbage
- 1 cup chayote, julienned thinly
- 1 cup cilantro
- ½ cup spring onion
- 10 cups chicken broth
- Lime
- 1 red chili pepper, sliced thinly and seeded

Directions:
1. Cook the rice noodles and divide it into 5 bowls.
2. Arrange the rest of ingredients on top of the rice noodles except for the broth.
3. Boil the broth and pour over the bowls. Serve with lime and red chili pepper.

Egg Pho Chay (Vegetable Pho with Egg)

Nutritional facts per serving:
Calories: 137 kcal
Fat: 4.4g
Protein: 3.7g
Carbohydrates: 14g
Fiber: less than 1g

Ingredients:
- 300g rice noodles, thin
- 1 kohirabi, peeled and julienned thinly
- 1 cup mung bean sprouts, blanched
- 2 cups chopped cilantro
- 1 cup onion
- ½ cup green onion
- 2 egg yolks
- dried pepper flakes (optional)
- 6 cups of vegetable pho broth
- Lime
- hoisin sauce
- chili sauce

Directions:
1. Divide the cooked noodles in 4 equal parts. Put each part in a bowl. Arrange the kohlrabi, sprouts, cilantro onion, and green onion on top of the rice noodles. (Note: If kohlrabi is not available, you can use turnip instead.) Leave a hole in the middle of the noodles in the bowl.
2. Drop the egg yolks carefully into the hole. Put a dash of pepper flakes on the yolks, if desired.
3. Reheat the broth. Pour it slowly from the side. Cover the bowls for a minute to poach the yolks. Serve with lime, chili sauce, and hoisin sauce.

Beef Tripe Pho

<u>Nutritional facts per serving:</u>
Calories: 243 kcal
Fat: 11g
Protein: 38g
Carbohydrates: 25g
Fiber: 1.2g

<u>Ingredients:</u>
- 1 kilo beef tripe
- ½ pound beef liver
- all ingredients for the Beef Pho Soup Base except for the beef shank
- 600g rice noodles, wide
- 1 cup red bell pepper
- 2 cups mung bean sprouts
- 2 cups cilantro
- 1 cup scallions
- ¼ cup green onion
- lime wedges
- hoisin sauce or chili garlic sauce
- black pepper

Directions:
1. Boil 16 cups of water in a large pot. Place the beef bones and the beef tripe. Simmer for 2 hours. Skim off the foam every 10 minutes.
2. Add 3 tablespoons of fish sauce and 1 tablespoon of salt. Add the toasted cardamom, star anise, cinnamon, and ginger.
3. Lift the tripe after two hours and poke with a fork to check if it is soft enough. Remove from heat. Slice into bite-size strips. Sprinkle with black pepper and set aside.
4. Put the beef liver into the pot along with the smashed shallots. Boil for 20 to 30 minutes or until the liver is soft when poked with a

fork. Turn off the heat. Remove the liver and slice it into bite size strips.

5. Arrange the tripe and liver on top of the cooked rice noodles. Add the bean sprouts, cilantro, red peppers, and the onions.

6. Pour the broth through a strainer to remove the bones and the other solid remnants from the tripe. Add the broth to each bowl of noodles. Serve with lime and choice of condiments. Eat hot.

Pho Bo Chay

Nutritional facts per serving:
Calories: 313 kcal
Fat: 14g
Protein: 27g
Carbohydrates: 27g
Fiber: 1.8g

Ingredients:
- 300 grams rice noodles, wide
- ½ pound or 1 bunch of Chinese broccoli
- ½ pound sirloin beef, cut into thin strips
- 1 tablespoon oyster sauce
- Sesame seeds
- 1 cup cilantro
- 1 cup scallions
- ¼ cup green onions
- Lime
- Tabasco sauce
- 8 cups beef pho broth

Directions:
1. Steam the broccoli until softer but still a little bit crunchy. Chop roughly and set aside.

2. Divide the cooked noodles into 5 bowls. Arrange the strips of beef and chopped broccoli on top of the rice noodles. Add the combined onion and cilantro. Put equal amounts of scallions on each bowl.
3. Boil the broth and add the oyster sauce. Pour the boiling broth into the bowl. Serve with lime and Tabasco sauce.

It Pho Ga (Less Soup Rice Noodle)

Nutritional facts per serving:
Calories: 288 kcal
Fat: 2g
Protein: 27g
Carbohydrates: 42g
Fiber: 3g

Ingredients:
- 400 grams rice noodles, thin
- 2 chicken breasts, cooked and chopped
- 1 cup shrimp, peeled, deveined and chopped
- 1 cup chayote
- 1 cup yellow cabbage
- 1 red pepper, sliced
- 1 cup onion
- 1 cup cilantro
- 1 tablespoon baked or fried garlic chips, chopped
- 4 to 6 cups of chicken soup
- black pepper
- lime
- oyster sauce

Directions:
1. Distribute cooked rice noodles into 4 to 6 bowls. Arrange the chicken breasts, shrimps, and vegetables on top of the rice noodles.

34

2. Boil the chicken base soup. Add the oyster sauce and the garlic chips. Bring to a quick boil and pour 1 cup of soup into bowls. Serve with lime.

Vegan Pho Noodles

Spiced Tofu and Mushroom Pho

Nutritional facts per serving:
Calories: 193 kcal
Fat: 2g
Protein: 14g
Carbohydrates: 33g
Fiber: 1.3g

Ingredients:
- 1 400 grams block of tofu
- ¼ teaspoon ngoyong or Chinese five spice
- Dash of black pepper
- Salt
- 1 scallion, sliced thinly
- 1 200 grams mushrooms, sliced
- 300 grams rice noodles, wide
- 2 cups cilantro
- ¼ cup green onions
- 1 green chili pepper, sliced thinly
- 6 cup of vegetable pho base
- vegetable oil
- lime slices

Directions:
1. Sprinkle salt on the tofu. Leave it for 30 minutes. Press the tofu between two wax paper sheets to remove excess liquid. Sprinkle ngoyong and black pepper on all sides of the tofu. Quarter the block and slice each quarter ½" thick.
2. Heat about ½ cup of oil in a skillet. Fry the tofu on each side in medium heat until the sides are golden.
3. Remove the excess vegetable oil from the skillet. Sauté the scallion for 2 minutes. Add the mushrooms and cook in medium fire for 5 minutes. Set aside.
4. Divide the cooked noodles in 5 servings. Arrange equal amounts of tofu, mushroom, cilantro, lime slices, and green onion on top of the rice noodles.
5. Reheat the broth. Pour it on the prepared bowls. Serve with soy sauce or Tabasco sauce.

Vietnamese Vegetable Pho

Nutritional facts per serving:
Calories: 153 kcal
Fat: 2g
Protein: 6g
Carbohydrates: 34g
Fiber: 2.7g

Ingredients:
- 300 grams rice noodles, wide
- 6 to 8 cups of vegetable pho base
- 1 medium kohlrabi, peeled and julienned thinly
- 1 medium daikon radish, peeled and sliced into thin rounds
- 1 medium sponge gourd, peeled and sliced into thin rounds
- 1 cup red onion
- 2 cups cilantro

- 1 bunch spring onion, chopped finely
- lime, sliced into almost paper thin wedges
- soy sauce and pepper

Directions:

1. Bring the vegetable pho base to a boil. Drop all the vegetables except for the spring onions. Boil for 1 minute and simmer for 3 minutes.
2. Add the rice noodles and turn off the heat. Leave for a minute for the heat to cook the noodles.
3. Scoop the noodle soup into 4 to 6 bowls. Make sure to add about the same amount of vegetables and noodle to each bowl.
4. Place lime wedges on the soup and top with spring onions. Serve with soy sauce and pepper.

Poor Man's Pho

Nutritional facts per serving:
Calories: 125 kcal
Fat: less than 1g
Protein: 2g
Carbohydrates: 29g
Fiber: 1.4g

Ingredients:
- 400 grams rice noodles, wide
- 10 cups of vegetable pho soup base
- 1 onion
- ½ cup spring onions
- 1 cup basil, roughly chopped
- 1 cup cilantro, roughly chopped

Directions:

1. Prepare the rice noodles as instructed and distribute it among 6 bowls.

2. Top it with beef onion, spring onions, basil, and cilantro. Pour the boiling broth into each bowl and serve the Pho with vinegar.

Quick Vegetable Pho

Nutritional facts per serving:
Calories: 147 kcal
Fat: 2g
Protein: 4g
Carbohydrates: 29g
Fiber: 1g

Ingredients:
- garlic about 2 fingers in size
- 1 large onion
- 2 cloves garlic
- 2 star anise
- 1 cinnamon stick
- 300 grams rice noodles, thin
- 1 cup mushroom, sliced
- 1 medium long sponge gourd, peeled and sliced in rounds
- 8 cups water
- ¼ cup spring onion
- 2 teaspoon olive oil
- salt and pepper
- light soy sauce
- lime
- 1 inch chunk of rock sugar or 1 tablespoon of light brown sugar

Directions:

1. Peel the ginger and slice into rounds. Place in a baking sheet, together with the star anise and cinnamon stick. Roast for 10 minutes. Set aside.
2. Add the oil and sauté the onion for 3 minutes over medium fire. Stir in the garlic and cook for another 2 minutes. Take half of the ginger rounds and sauté with the onions. Add the mushrooms and sprinkle a pinch of salt and pepper. Sauté for 5 minutes.
3. Add the water, 3 tablespoons of soy sauce, rock sugar, and 1 tablespoon of salt. Bring to a quick boil. Drop the cinnamon and star anise. Simmer for 20 minutes.
4. Add the sponge gourd and bring the broth to a quick boil. Turn off the heat and add the rice noodles. Cover for 1 minute to allow the noodles to cook. Ladle into bowls. Top with spring onion and serve with lime. Makes 4 to 6.

Zucchini Pho

Nutritional facts per serving:
Calories: 111 kcal
Fat: less than 1g
Protein: 1g
Carbohydrates: 22g
Fiber: 5.6g

Ingredients:
- 300g zucchini
- 100g cucumber
- 150g carrots, peeled and thinly julienned
- 150g turnip, peeled and thinly julienned
- 100g pear, peeled and thinly julienned
- 1 cup cilantro, roughly chopped
- 1 cup yellow onion, sliced
- 1 cup shitake mushroom, chopped (optional)

- ngoyong spiced tofu or Asian flavored tofu, cubed
- 1 tablespoon rice vinegar
- 6 cups vegetable pho base
- olive oil

Directions:

1. Cut the zucchini lengthwise. Brush with oil and arrange in a baking sheet, face down. Bake in a 200C preheated oven for 20 minutes. Leave them to cool to touch. Peel and cut into long, thin noodle strips. Divide into 4 bowls.
2. Divide the vegetables and tofu equally and place in each bowl.
3. Reheat the soup. When it is near its boiling point, add the rice vinegar, and the shitake mushroom, if using. Boil for 5 minutes. Pour into the bowls. Serve with chili garlic sauce.

Calabash (Bottle Gourd) and Sprouts Pho

Nutritional facts per serving:
Calories: 173 kcal
Fat: 1g
Protein: 7g
Carbohydrates: 26g
Fiber: 3.8g

Ingredients:

- 1 cup calabash, peeled and chunked
- 1 cup bean sprouts
- 1 small tomato, diced
- 2 cloves garlic, minced
- 1 large yellow onion, sliced
- 1 cup bok choy leaves or spinach
- 300 grams rice noodles, wide
- 1 thin slice of licorice roots
- 1 cinnamon stick

- 2 star anise
- 2 bay leaf
- 3 tablespoon soy sauce
- 1 tablespoon sesame oil
- 1 tablespoon olive oil
- 8 cups water
- 2 large onion, halved
- 5 leeks, white part only, halved
- 1 large carrots, cut into large chunks
- 2 stalks celery, cut into chunks
- ginger, about the size of three fingers, smashed

Directions:

1. Boil the water in a pot. Add the carrots, halved onion, leeks, and celery. Simmer for 15 minutes.
2. Toast the licorice, anise, and cinnamon in a pan for 2 minutes. Rinse. Add to the pot, together with the ginger. Simmer for another 15 minutes.
3. Place another pot over medium heat. Sauté the sliced onion for three minutes. Add the garlic and cook for another minute. Stir in the tomato and cook for 5 minutes.
4. Add the calabash and cook for 5 minutes or until the calabash is tender. Pour in a little bit of broth to keep it from sticking from the pot. Stir in the bean sprouts and cook for another minute.
5. Strain the broth and add to the calabash mixture. Boil. Add the bok choy leaves and sesame oil.
6. Turn off the heat and add the rice noodles. Let it stand for a minute while covered before scooping into bowls. Serves 5 to 6.

Spicy Vegan Pho

Nutritional facts per serving:
Calories: 177kcal
Fat: 4g
Protein: 8g
Carbohydrates: 33g
Fiber: 1.9g

Ingredients:
- 300 grams rice noodles
- 1 cup mung bean sprouts
- 1 cup yellow cabbage
- 1 cup scallions, sliced
- 1 to 2 teaspoons chili paste
- 1 cup chopped cilantro
- ¼ cup green onions
- 1 250g pack Asian flavored tofu sheets
- ¼ cup shitake mushroom, chopped
- 8 cups of vegetable pho base
- lime, sliced thinly crosswise
- 1 green chili, sliced thinly, seeds removed

Directions:
1. Divide the cooked rice noodles into 4 to 6 bowls. Chop the tofu sheets roughly and arrange it in the bowl. Arrange the cilantro and scallions.
2. Boil the vegetable pho base. Add the chili paste and shitake mushroom. Simmer for 5 minutes. Add the cabbage, green onions, and bean sprouts. Turn off the heat.
3. Strain the broth and set aside. Divide the mushroom and vegetables into the bowls. Pour the hot broth over the noodles. Top with slices of lime and green chili.

Tay Pho

<u>Nutritional facts per serving:</u>
Calories: 101kcal
Fat: 4g
Protein: 1g
Carbohydrates: 21g
Fiber: 1g

<u>Ingredients:</u>
- 300 grams noodles, wide or zucchini noodles
- 1 cup scallions, sliced
- 1 cup yellow onion, sliced
- ½ cup spring onion, chopped
- ¼ cup cilantro, chopped
- lime, sliced crosswise
- chili garlic sauce
- 2 tablespoon apple-cider vinegar
- 8 cups vegetable pho base
- 1 teaspoon sesame oil
- 1 tablespoon coconut oil
- green or red chili peppers, sliced

Directions:
1. Sauté the yellow onion in coconut oil for 5 minutes. Reduce the fire to low. Continue stirring until the onion caramelizes. Set aside.
2. Cook the rice noodles or zucchini noodles and divide into 5 or 6 bowls.
3. Arrange the caramelized onions, scallions, green onions, and cilantro on top of the noodles.
4. Reheat the broth and add the apple-cider vinegar. Bring to a boil and simmer for 5 minutes. Pour over the noodles. Top with chili peppers and lime slices.

Winter Pho Chay

<u>Nutritional facts per serving:</u>
Calories: 135kcal
Fat: 4g
Protein: 6g
Carbohydrates: 21g
Fiber: 5.6g

<u>Ingredients:</u>
- 300g rice noodles, wide or thin
- 1 medium parsnip
- 1 medium turnip
- 1 small head of cauliflower
- 1 medium carrots
- 1 cup chopped yellow cabbage
- 8 cups of water
- 3 tablespoon of soy sauce
- ginger, about the size of 2 fingers, smashed
- 2 large scallions, smashed
- 2 star anise
- 1 licorice root
- 2 bay leaf
- 1 tablespoon salt
- 1 tablespoon light brown sugar
- 1 teaspoon sesame oil
- ½ cup cilantro, roughly chopped

Directions:
1. Boil the water in a deep pot. Place the ginger, star anise, licorice root, and smashed scallion in a tea cloth or bag. Put in the water and simmer for 10 minutes. Add the soy sauce, sugar, and salt. Continue to simmer for 5 minutes.

2. Peel the root vegetables and cut into 1" chunks. Add to the simmering water. Cook for 15 minutes or until the soft.

3. Save the teabag for future use. Add the cabbage and the cilantro to the pot. Cook for a minute. Stir in the rice noodles and sesame oil. Turn off the heat. Serve with extra onions and chili sauce on the side.

Sour Vegetable Pho

Nutritional facts per serving:
Calories: 146kcal
Fat: 2g
Protein: 4g
Carbohydrates: 17g
Fiber: 3.3g

Ingredients:
- 300g rice noodles, wide
- 2 tablespoons tamarind paste or fresh tamarind meat
- 24 young okra, slice in half
- 1 cup mung bean sprouts
- ½ cup onion, sliced
- 3 medium tomatoes, quartered
- 8 cups vegetable pho base
- salt and pepper
- ½ cup cilantro, chopped

Directions:
1. Reheat the broth. Stir in the tamarind paste. Add the okra and bring to a quick boil. Lower the fire and simmer for 10 minutes or until the okra is tender.
2. Divide the cooked noodles in 5 to 6 bowls.

3. Arrange the tomatoes, onion, cilantro, and sprouts on top of the noodles. Scoop some okra from the pot and place it with the rest of the vegetables.

4. Pour the soup over the noodles. Serve with chili paste or sliced chili peppers on the side.

Pho with a Twist

Imperial Beef Noodle Soup

<u>Nutritional facts per serving:</u>
Calories: 527kcal
Fat: 14g
Protein: 37g
Carbohydrates: 53g
Fiber: 4.1g

<u>For the Braised Beef:</u>
- ½ kilo beef brisket, cut into 1½" cubes
- 1 large onion, sliced
- 1 teaspoon pepper
- ¼ teaspoon ngoyong or Chinese five spice
- ½ teaspoon salt
- 1 cup mushroom
- 2 cups of the basic Pho base
- 1 tables spoon olive oil
- 1 teaspoon flour

<u>For the Pho:</u>
- 400 grams rice spaghetti, or regular rice noodles
- 1 cup cilantro, chopped finely
- ½ cup green onions
- lime, sliced thinly

- 8 cups of the basic Pho base

Directions:

1. Sauté the onion until it caramelizes. Add the flour and stir quickly. Reduce the fire to medium before adding the broth. Stir.
2. Add the beef cubes and season with salt, pepper, and ngoyong. Increase the heat to bring the broth to a quick boil. Reduce to medium-low and simmer for one hour. Add more broth, if necessary.
3. Add the mushrooms and cook until the broth is reduce to a saucy texture. Remove from fire.
4. Cook the rice spaghetti or noodles according to package. Distribute to 6 to 8 bowls.
5. Divide the braised beef to the number of bowls. Mix the cilantro and green onions and place them on top of the noodles and beef.
6. Reheat the pho broth and pour in the prepared bowls.

Pork Feet Ginseng Pho

Nutritional facts per serving:
Calories: 423kcal
Fat: 17g
Protein: 19g
Carbohydrates: 31g
Fiber: 3.5g

Ingredients:

- 1 kilo pig feet or 2 feet, cleaned well
- Salt
- ¼ kilo leeks, white part only
- 2 thumb-size ginseng root, smashed
- 1 cup cilantro
- ½ cup spring onion
- 1 cup onion

- 12 cups of chicken pho base
- ¼ cup sweet vinegar or apple-cider vinegar
- 400g rice noodles, wide
- 1 cup button mushrooms, halved
- 1 medium radish, cut in rounds
- 1 medium carrots, cut in rounds

Directions:

1. Boil water in a deep pot. Make sure that it can cover the pig feet. Rub a handful of salt to the feet. Rinse quickly in tap water before putting them in the boiling water. Boil for 15 minutes.
2. Boil the chicken Pho base. Add the smash ginseng and leeks and boil for 5 minutes. Add the pig feet and simmer for 1½ hours or until the feet are tender.
3. Stir in the vinegar. Bring to a boil. Correct the taste with salt and fish sauce.
4. Add the radish and carrots. Cook for 10 minutes or until the vegetables are tender.
5. Remove the pig feet and the leeks. Chop the feet into serving pieces. Mince the ginseng.
6. Cook the rice noodles and divide it into 5 to 8 bowls. Scoop some radish and carrots into the bowl. Arrange the pork over the noodles. Top each bowl with mixed onion, green onion and cilantro.
7. Fill the bowl with the broth. Add small amounts of ginseng to each bowl. Serve with lime and sliced chili.

Mexican Influenced Pho

Nutritional facts per serving:
Calories: 489kcal
Fat: 12g
Protein: 27g
Carbohydrates: 57g
Fiber: 4.4g

Ingredients:

- 300g rice noodles, wide or fresh ramen noodles
- 1 rib eye steak (160 to 200 grams)
- Salt and pepper
- 1 garlic clove
- 1 yellow pepper, sliced
- 1 red pepper, sliced
- ½ cup onion
- ½ cup cilantro
- ½ cup green onion
- 1 medium carrots, julienned
- 1 jalapeno, sliced thinly
- lime, sliced into thin wedges
- 8 cups beef pho base or basic pho base
- 1 teaspoon sriracha
- 1 tablespoon sesame oil
- 1 tablespoon roasted peanuts, chopped (optional)

Directions:

1. Cook the noodles according to the package instruction or as instructed in preceding recipes. Drizzle with sesame oil and mix. Divide into 4 to 6 bowls.
2. Smash the garlic clove and rub onto the steak. Sprinkle salt and pepper on each side. Grill in a little oil on medium heat for 3

minutes on each side. Slice thinly and arrange on top of the noodles.

3. Arrange the onion, carrots, jalapeno, and sweet peppers on the bowl. Mix the cilantro and green onion. Sprinkle them on top of the veggies in the bowl.

4. Reheat the broth and pour over the noodles. Top with chopped peanuts. Serve with lime, hoisin sauce and additional jalapenos.

Bat Choy (Filipino Style Pho)

Nutritional facts per serving:
Calories: 421kcal
Fat: 17g
Protein: 23g
Carbohydrates: 29g
Fiber: 2g

Ingredients:
- 400g rice noodles, thin or thin ramen noodles
- 12 cups basic Pho base
- 1 cup scallions
- ¼ kilo pork, stomach part
- ¼ kilo pork intestine, cleaned well
- ¼ kilo pork liver
- ½ cup green onion
- ½ cup cilantro
- 2 stalks lemon grass
- salt and pepper
- vegetable oil for deep frying

Directions:
1. Score the skin of the pork. Rub with salt. Set aside for 10 minutes.

2. Place the intestines and liver in a deep pot. Cover with water. Add a little salt and lemon grass. Bring to a quick boil and simmer for 2 hours.

3. Heat the oil in a deep frying pan. Deep fry the pork for 10 minutes. Place on a rack and cool while waiting for the intestines to cook. Do not discard the oil.

4. Divide the noodles into 5 bowls. When the innards are cooked, cut them into thin slices. Place them on top of the cooked noodles.

5. Reheat the oil. Deep fry the pork for another 10 minutes to make it crispy. Separate the skin and fat from the meat. Slice the pork thinly and place on top of the noodles.

6. Top with onion, cilantro, and green onions. Reheat the broth and pour over the noodles.

7. Chop the crispy fat and skin. Sprinkle on top of the soup before serving. Serve with soy sauce and pepper.

Boiled Down Tofu over Pho

Nutritional facts per serving:
Calories: 210kcal
Fat: 8g
Protein: 27g
Carbohydrates: 25g
Fiber: 1.7g

Ingredients:
- 1 200g block tofu
- 300g rice noodles
- 1 tablespoon chili powder
- 2 tablespoons honey
- 1 teaspoon soy sauce
- 1 large onion, sliced
- 1 clove garlic, minced
- 2 tablespoon sweet vinegar or apple-cider vinegar

- 1 teaspoon sesame oil
- 8 cups vegetable pho base
- ½ cup cilantro
- ½ cup spring onion
- 1 cup bean sprouts, blanched
- oil for frying (optional)
- salt and pepper

Directions:
1. Slice the tofu into squares. Sprinkle with salt and pepper. Fry over medium heat until the sides become golden brown. (Optional)
2. Place the tofu in a sauce pan. Add the onion. Mix the sesame oil, soy sauce, vinegar, chili powder, honey and a little water. Taste. Drizzle over the tofu. Bring to a quick boil. Reduce the heat and simmer in low heat until the sauce thickens.
3. Cook the noodles according to package directions and divide into 4 to 6 bowls. Place the bean sprouts on one side of the bowl. Arrange the tofu on the other side. Sprinkle with mixed cilantro and green onions.
4. Reheat the stock and pour over the noodles. Serve with lime, hoisin sauce or honey.

Ravioli in Pho Broth

Nutritional facts per serving:
Calories: 358kcal
Fat: 15g
Protein: 32g
Carbohydrates: 14g
Fiber: less than 1g

Ingredients:
- 100g 90% ground beef
- 50g shitake mushroom, chopped finely

- 1 small scallion, chopped finely
- salt and pepper
- 50g spinach, blanched and chopped roughly
- 1 egg, separated
- wanton wrappers
- ½ cup cilantro
- ½ cup spring onion
- ¼ cup onion, sliced
- Oil
- 5 cups chicken Pho broth
- fried garlic chips, crushed

Directions:

1. Heat about a teaspoon of oil over medium heat. Sauté the finely chopped scallion for a minute. Add the mushrooms and cook for two minutes before adding the beef. Season with salt and pepper. Cook until the beef changes color. Stir in the spinach.
2. Cool down. Add the egg yolk to gather the ingredients. Set aside.
3. Add a pinch of salt to the flour and mix thoroughly. Make a well in the middle and put the eggs. Whisk the eggs until frothy and slowly incorporate the flour until the mixture is well combined.
4. Lay a wanton wrapper on a plate or prepping board. Place about a tablespoon of filling in the center. Brush the sides with egg whites and cover with another sheet. Make about 5 to 8 ravioli for each bowl. Arrange on each bowl. Sprinkle with mixed cilantro and green onions.
5. Boil the broth and scoop slowly into each bowl until the ravioli is covered. Do not pour straight on the ravioli or it will burst. Serve with fried garlic on top.

Sour and Spicy Pho

Nutritional facts per serving:
Calories: 262kcal
Fat: 8g
Protein: 17g
Carbohydrates: 25g
Fiber: 1.2g

Ingredients:

- 300g rice noodles, thick
- Meat from the beef shank used in the broth
- 2 tablespoons miso paste
- 1 tablespoons chili paste
- 1 small head of Napa cabbage
- ½ cup red bell pepper
- 8 cups basic pho base
- ½ cup onion
- 1 cup cilantro
- Lime wedges
- Chili peppers
- Olive oil

Directions:

1. Divide the cooked noodles into 4 to 6 bowls. Remove the bone from the shank and chop the meat. Arrange on top of the rice noodles.
2. Heat a little amount of oil. Sauté the yellow cabbage for 2 minutes over medium heat. Add equal amounts each bowl. Place the onions, cilantro, and red bell pepper into the bowl. Cut one chili pepper in half and place on one side of each bowl.
3. Reheat the broth. Add the miso paste and chili paste. Bring to a boil for 5 minutes. Ladle the broth into the prepared bowls. Serve with lime juice.

Phorridge

<u>Nutritional facts per serving:</u>
Calories: 211kcal
Fat: 7g
Protein: 14g
Carbohydrates: 24g
Fiber: 1g

<u>Ingredients:</u>
- ½ cup uncooked long grain rice, washed
- 1 cup mushrooms, chopped
- ½ cup cilantro chopped
- ½ cup onion sliced
- 1 cup shredded chicken breast
- 8 cups chicken Pho base
- salt and pepper
- lime or vinegar
- oil

Directions:
1. Heat oil in a deep saucepan. Sauté the onion on medium heat for 3 minutes. Add the rice and sauté for five minutes.
2. Add 4 cups of chicken broth. Bring to a quick boil and simmer on low heat for 1 hour or until the liquid is reduce to half. Stir occasionally. When the liquid is reduced to half, stir the porridge continuously.
3. Add the mushrooms. Cook until the liquid is almost gone. Distribute the porridge into bowls. Makes 4 serving.
4. Top the porridge with chicken, cilantro and green onion. Add more broth to the porridge until the cilantro and green onion swims in broth. Serve with vinegar or lime wedges, hoisin sauce, soy sauce, and black pepper.

Other Vietnamese Noodle Soups

Duck Noodle Soup with Bamboo Shoots

Nutritional facts per serving:
Calories: 202kcal
Fat: 3g
Protein: 4g
Carbohydrates: 32g
Fiber: 1.6g

Ingredients:
- 1 whole duck, dressed
- 300g rice spaghetti or regular egg noodles
- ¼ cup leeks, white only
- 3 shallots, peeled and smashed
- 2 ginger, about the size of 2 fingers
- 400g canned bamboo shoots
- ½ cup onion, sliced thinly
- ½ cup chopped mint
- ½ cup chopped cilantro
- ½ cup chopped basil
- 6 cups chicken stock (you may use regular chicken Pho base)
- 1 red chili pepper chopped
- Salt

- oil

Directions:

1. Peel and smash one of the gingers. Rub it all over the duck skin and inside the skin. Get a handful of salt and rub it all over the duck. Rinse thoroughly. Place the smashed shallots and the other smashed ginger in the cavity of the duck.

2. Put water (enough to cover the duck) in a pot. Boil. Add the duck and the leeks. Cook in low heat for one hour. Remove the duck and get the duck breast. Chop it into chunks and set aside.

3. Cook the noodles according to the package instructions. Divide it into 5 bowls.

4. Arrange the duck meat in the bowl. Drain the water from the bamboo shoots. Rinse and squeeze the excess water. Add on top of the noodles.

5. Combine the herbs and the onions. Place them on top of the noodles.

6. Remove the leeks from the duck broth. Add the chicken stock and wait until the broth is briskly boiling. Pour into the prepared bowls. Serve with fish sauce with slices of chili peppers.

Bun Bo Hue

Nutritional facts per serving:
Calories: 522kcal
Fat: 21g
Protein: 37g
Carbohydrates: 33g
Fiber: less than 1g

Ingredients:

- 2 kilo beef bones
- 1 kilo beef shank
- ½ kilo pork shoulders
- 500g thick egg noodles or any thick noodles

- 1 cup pork blood (optional or can be replaced with 100g tofu sheets)
- 1 teaspoon dried chili pepper flakes
- 1 tablespoon annatto seeds
- ¼ cup coconut oil
- 1 cup basil
- 1 cup cilantro
- 1 cup mint
- ¼ kilo lemon grass
- 3 large stalks of leeks, white part only
- 1 cup onion
- salt

Directions:

1. Place the bones, shank, lemon grass, and leeks in a pot. Cover with about 16 cups of water. Bring to a quick boil. Reduce the fire to low and simmer for 1 hour.
2. Add the pork shoulder and simmer for another hour. Strain the broth and set aside. Chop the meat from the shank and the pork shoulder.
3. In a small saucepan, heat the oil over low fire. Add the annatto seeds and stir until the oil changes the color. Add the chili pepper flakes and sauté on low heat until for 2 minutes. Strain the oil. Add the oil to the boiling broth.
4. If using pork blood, boil a cup of water in a saucepan. Add the pork blood. Do not stir. Bring to a boil until the blood coagulates. Cut into thin slices.
5. Cook the noodles according to package directions and divide into 8 to 10 bowls. Arrange the beef and pork on top of the noodles. Add the coagulated blood or tofu sheets. Mix the onion and the herbs. Put them in the bowl.
6. Pour the chili broth into each bowl of noodles. Serve with lime and hot sauce.

Bun Riu or Tomato Noodle Soup

Nutritional facts per serving:
Calories: 227kcal
Fat: 10g
Protein: 17g
Carbohydrates: 34g
Fiber: 2.6g

Ingredients:

- 2 cup fresh tomatoes, chunked
- 2 tablespoons shrimp or crab paste
- 1 tablespoon tamarind paste
- 400 grams vermicelli noodles or rice noodles
- 3 red chili peppers
- 1 teaspoon annatto oil
- 1 large onion, sliced
- 200g tofu, fried to golden brown, cubed
- 200g pork chop, fried (salt and pepper only), cubed
- 100g cooked shrimps or crabmeat
- Mint
- salt and pepper

Directions:

1. Place a deep saucepan over medium heat. Add the annatto oil. Sauté the onion until it is translucent. Add the tomatoes and cook until the juice starts to come out.
2. Stir in the crab paste and the tamarind paste. Add 5 cups of water. Bring to a boil and simmer for 20 minutes. Skim the foam every 5 minutes. Add the chili peppers. Mix and turn off the heat.
3. Cook the noodles and divide it into 4 to 5 bowls. Arrange the pork, tofu, and shrimps on top of the noodles.
4. Ladle the thick tomato broth to the bowl. Serve with chopped mint on top.

Cucumber Noodle Soup

Nutritional facts per serving:
Calories: 198kcal
Fat: 6g
Protein: 4g
Carbohydrates: 29g
Fiber: 1g

Ingredients:

- 300 grams egg noodles or any round, thick noodles
- 2 medium cucumber, peeled and julienned
- 1 medium carrots, peeled and julienned
- 1 cup shredded cabbage
- ½ kilo pork tendon, sliced in sirloin strips
- 1 pork feet
- Cilantro
- green onion
- 1 large onion, halved
- 1 rock sugar or 1 tablespoon light brown sugar
- 3 tablespoons fish sauce

Directions:

1. Boil 2 cups of water. Rub salt on the pork feet and wash. Place in the boiling water. Add the pork tendon stips and turn off the heat. Let it stand for 5 minutes. Drain and rinse with tap water. Set aside.
2. Boil 8 cups of water in a deep pot. Add the pork feet, halved onion, brown sugar and fish sauce. Bring to a quick boil and simmer for 1 hour. Skim off the foam every 10 minutes.
3. Add the pork tendon strips and cook for 10 minutes. Add a dash of salt and pepper. Make sure that the broth only has a hint of saltiness and will not overpower the taste of the cucumber.
4. When the pork tendon is soft, remove the pork feet and onion. Debone and place the meat back into the pot. Add the carrots,

cucumber, cabbage, half of the cilantro, and half of the green onion.

5. Ladle the broth over the cooked noodles. Arrange the vegetables on top of the noodles. Serve with the fresh green onion and cilantro.

Rice Pasta with Pork and Shrimp Sticks

Nutritional facts per serving:
Calories: 221kcal
Fat: 8g
Protein: 12g
Carbohydrates: 34g
Fiber: 1g

Ingredients:
- 400 grams of rice pasta, macaroni shaped
- 1 medium radish, peeled
- 200 grams shrimps, peeled and deveined
- 200 grams ground pork
- 8 cups chicken stock or use the chicken pho base
- 1 large onion, sliced
- 1 scallion minced
- Salt and pepper
- a handful of cilantro mixed with a handful of mint, chopped
- 2 tablespoons fish sauce (omit if you are using the pho base)
- ½ teaspoon sugar
- 1 teaspoon potato starch
- 1 bunch of lettuce leaves
- 1 tablespoon sesame oil
- juice of 1 lime
- bread crumbs
- oil for frying

Directions:

1. Mince the shrimps. Mix in the ground pork, salt, pepper, and sugar. Add the starch and mix until incorporated well. Form into finger shape and size. Roll in bread crumbs and deep fry until golden brown. Set aside to drain the excess oil.

2. Boil the chicken stock. Cut the radish lengthwise and slice into thin half-moons. Add to the stock, together with the onion. Stir in the fish sauce and a dash of salt. Cook for 5 minutes.

3. Roughly chop the lettuce leaves. Drizzle with sesame oil and lime juice. Mix.

4. Scoop some cooked rice pasta in a bowl. Add a handful of lettuce salad and a few pieces of the pork sticks.

5. Pour some broth over the noodles and scoop some of the radish into the soup. Top with the chopped cilantro and mint mix. Serve. Makes 4 to 6 servings.

Pho and Noodle Partners

Vietnamese Spring Rolls

Nutritional facts per serving:
Calories: 121kcal
Fat: 2g
Protein: 9g
Carbohydrates: 28g
Fiber: 3g

Ingredients:
- 2 cups rice noodles, cooked and cut short
- 1 cup shrimp, deveined and chopped roughly
- ¼ cup basil, chopped finely
- ¼ cup cilantro, chopped finely
- ¼ cup shredded cabbage
- ¼ cup mint, chopped finely
- 3 tablespoons hoisin sauce
- 1 teaspoon peanuts, chopped finely
- 8 to 10 rice wrappers (8" in diameter)

Directions:
1. Combine the rice noodles, shrimp, and vegetables. In a small bowl, mix the hoisin sauce and peanuts. Place in a bottle with a piper.

2. Soak the wrappers in hot water for 30 seconds to 1 minute. Place in a non-stick surface or sheet. Put a handful of the filling. Pipe a small amount of hoisin-peanut mixture. Roll and seal the wrap.

Bahn Tieu (Hollow Donuts)

Nutritional facts per serving:
Calories: 239kcal (3 donuts)
Fat: 11g
Protein: 4g
Carbohydrates: 31g
Fiber: 4g

Ingredients:
- ½ cup hot water
- Sugar
- 1 cup all-purpose flour
- ½ teaspoon baking powder
- ½ teaspoon active dry yeast
- ½ teaspoon salt
- sesame seeds, black or white
- oil for frying

Directions:
1. Mix 1 tablespoon of sugar and hot water. Add the dry yeast and set aside for 10 minutes.
2. Mix the remaining dry ingredients in another bowl. Stir in the yeast mixture and incorporate well.
3. Knead the dough for 10 minutes or until it is shiny and pliable. Transfer to a clean bowl and cover with plastic wrap. Set aside for an hour.

4. Punch the dough to remove the air and roll it into a log. Divide the dough into 12 to 16 portions. Shape each portion into a bowl and roll in sesame seeds. Flatten the dough into ¼" rounds.

5. Heat the oil in medium fire. Drop the dough one by one into the oil. Wait until the bread floats and puffs. Flip the bread to brown the top part. Remove and drain the excess oil.

Quay or Fried Bread Sticks

Nutritional facts per serving:
Calories: 200kcal (5 sticks)
Fat: 13g
Protein: 0g
Carbohydrates: 15g
Fiber: less than 1g

Ingredients:
- 500g bread flour or all-purpose flour
- 2 teaspoons baking soda
- 1 teaspoon baking powder
- 300ml water
- 1 tablespoon sugar
- 1 teaspoon salt
- oil for frying

Directions:
1. Place the baking soda and baking powder in separate bowls. Add 50ml water to each agent.
2. In a mixing bowl, mix together the flour, sugar and salt. Make a well in the center and pour the baking soda water, baking powder water, and the plain water. (Follow the order.)
3. Mix until the ingredients gather into dough. Knead the dough for 5 minutes. Place in a clean bowl. Set it aside, uncovered, for 20 minutes.

4. Knead the dough again for 2 minutes. Set aside to rest for another 20 minutes. Repeat this step until the dough becomes smooth. Place the smooth dough in a clean bowl. Cover with plastic wrap and let it rise for 3 hours.
5. Transfer the dough to the kneading surface. Knead for a minute. Roll into a ¼" thick sheet. Cut the dough into 3" by 1" strips. Set aside. You can sprinkle chili powder or black pepper on the strips to make the bread spicy.
6. Fry the bread sticks the same way as the Bahn Tieu.

Steamed Sweet Rice Cake

Nutritional facts per serving:
Calories: 165kcal
Fat: 2g
Protein: 9g
Carbohydrates: 30g
Fiber: 3g

Ingredients:
- 2 cups cake flour or rice flour
- 300ml water
- ¼ cup tapioca starch
- 1 teaspoon active dry yeast
- 1 teaspoon salt
- 1½ teaspoon double acting baking powder
- 1 can condensed milk (1 cup)
- 1 teaspoon vanilla

Directions:
1. Combine all the dry ingredients in a bowl. Add the water. Whisk thoroughly. Let it rest for 1 hour.
2. Mix the condensed milk with vanilla and pour to the flour mixture. Incorporate well.

3. Transfer the batter in muffin pans or steamer-proof cups. Steam for 15 minutes. Make sure to cover the lid of the steamer with cheese cloth, so to avoid the steam from falling into the cake. Serve. A great partner for spicy soups.

Banh Goi or Crispy Dumplings

Nutritional facts per serving:
Calories: 264kcal (2 dumplings)
Fat: 17g
Protein: 11g
Carbohydrates: 49g
Fiber: 11g

Ingredients:
- 1 cup flour
- ½ teaspoon salt
- 1 teaspoon sugar
- 1 teaspoon baking powder
- 150ml water
- ½ kilo pork cubes
- 100g shrimp, peeled and deveined
- 50g mushroom
- ¼ cup spring onion, finely chopped
- ½ cup carrots, minced
- salt and pepper
- 1 teaspoon fish sauce
- hard boiled eggs, chopped (optional)
- oil for frying

Directions:
1. Place the pork cubes, shrimp, mushroom, fish sauce, salt, pepper and dash of sugar in a food processor. Grind until well incorporated.

2. Transfer to a bowl. Fold in the onion and carrots. Set aside.

3. Combine the first five ingredients to make the dough. Knead until it is pliable. Roll into 1/8" inch sheet. Cut in 4" circles.

4. Place some filling at the center of wrapper. Fold the edges to make a half-moon shape dumpling. Secure the edges.

5. Deep fry the dumplings in medium heat until golden brown. Serve as a partner for pho or with chili or hoisin sauce.

CONCLUSION

Congratulations! You now have more than just a handful of creative yet easy-to-make Pho recipes. I hope that you enjoyed reading through the recipes in this book and that you have realized how flexible Pho is as a healthy and flavorful dish. When you have gotten the hang of cooking the recipes in this book, you can experiment and get creative with your own concoctions. You simply have to make the Pho broth base and then put together your own combination of ingredients.

The level of difficulty of the 50 Pho Noodle Soups and Side Dishes Recipes in this book is Easy. That's why you cannot go wrong with these recipes even if you are a beginner. You can go at your own pace and try out the recipes that you feel comfortable with. Or, you can choose to make the recipes with ingredients that are familiar to you or that are available in your local produce market.

Have fun with your Pho!

Did you find this book helpful? I would appreciate your honest review!

Why I'm asking for reviews:

Reader reviews are the key to an author's success!

Thank you for your support!

Yours truly,

Mathias Müller

AUTHOR

Pho, full flavor - in this wonderful cookbook Mathias Müller explains over 50 basic recipes in detail. Müller's clear-cut, passionate writing not only inspire novices to follow their intuition in the kitchen and understand the essence of a recipe: 'Honestly, good food is nothing more than good ingredients prepared simply'. There are lots of delicious and easy recipes for a healthy diet to cook for any meal.

'HEALTHY LIVING' is Müller's philosophy which comes to life in every line of this new edition of the classic "The Pho Cookbook: 50 Easy to Creative Recipes for Vietnam's Favorite Soup and Noodles". Müller has published various bestsellers:

"Low Carb Recipes - 50 Lunch Recipes for Successful Weight Loss in Just 2 Weeks"

"Low Carb Recipes – 50 Dinners for Permanent Weight Loss Success"

"Low Carb Recipes - 50 Vegetarian and Vegan Recipes for Successful Weight Loss in Just 2 Weeks"

"Low Carb Recipes – 14-Day Plan with Delicious Recipes for Permanent Weight Loss at Home and on the Road"

"Low Carb Recipes - 100 Low Carb breakfast recipes for successful weight loss in 2 weeks"

"Low Carb Recipes - 100 Low Carb Desserts for Successful Weight Loss in 2 Weeks"

"Low Carb Recipes – 300 Low Carb Recipes for Permanent Weight Loss Success"

"Paleo Recipes: 50 delicious Paleo Breakfast Recipes for Permanent Weight Loss at Home and on the Road"

Made in the USA
Las Vegas, NV
30 April 2024

89333830R00046